SOUTHERN ELECTRIC SLAM-DOOR STOCK
The Final Years

Roger Palmer

Ian Allan

PUBLISHING

Introduction

Introduced in 1956 to replace steam on the Kent Coast main line and the routes through Maidstone East to Ashford, Margate, Folkestone and Dover, the '4-CEPs' continued thundering up and down for more than 30 years, until many were transferred to work services out of Waterloo. Alan Williams, that well-respected commentator of the contemporary railway, was singularly scathing and totally unimpressed by their design, this being merely a standard Mk 1 coach with a couple of windows punched in one end and the gangway-end adapted to take a regulation Southern Region two-character head-code panel. And, until they were fitted with Commonwealth bogies, they were extremely rough riders, giving rise to a volley of complaints from passengers, as well as the advice to ensure one's suit was the same colour as the soup when lunching in the buffet cars of the '4-BEPs'!

The '4-CIGs', introduced from 1964, came under the same sort of flak. They were built to replace the prewar units used on the Brighton line and were perhaps a smoothed-out and tidied-up version of the earlier '4-CEPs', with glassfibre front ends with recessed panels for the brake jumper and control cables and rounded at the top to blend into the roof line. In the early 1970s later builds of '4-CIGs' replaced prewar units of '4-BUF' and '4-COR' types on the Reading line, the Sussex Coast lines to/from Victoria and London Bridge and between Portsmouth and Waterloo/Victoria, as well as on 'Coastway' services. They also made frequent appearances on the Bournemouth line, which was more commonly associated with the visually similar '4-REPs' and '4-TCs' designed for use on those trains that hammered up and down the South Western main line to Bournemouth following steam's demise in 1967. The '4-CIGs' could be worked coupled to the '4-CEPs' and '4-VEPs' — the latter, high-density stock introduced from 1967 for semi-fast services but which could in fact end up working fast express trains.

Writing in 1977, Alan Williams quotes a railwayman colleague as describing a 'VEP' as "a '4-SUB' with corridors". Williams' main complaint lay more in the æsthetics and in the lack of air-conditioning, which featured in contemporary coaching stock being built for services north of the Thames; what he would think of the situation at the beginning of the 21st century, when the '4-CEPs', '4-CIGs' and '4-VEPs' represented the last survivors of traditional 'slam-door' stock is, of course, open to speculation. A survey carried out towards the end of 2003 to assess the comparative reliability of the various unit types

---

Front cover: When trains terminated at **Haslemere** through the middle part of the day it was possible to photograph a combination of any two of '4-CIG', '4-VEP' or '4-CEP' standing side-by-side, because one of the limited-stop trains would pay a call just a few minutes after the terminating service had arrived. Here, showing the front-end differences between the '4-CEPs' and the later '4-CIGs', are '4-CIG' No 1887 on the 14.40 return working to Waterloo and '4-CEP' No 1581 on the 13.38 Waterloo–Portsmouth Harbour on 23 April 2004. *Roger Palmer*

Back cover: On what had been a blisteringly hot day '4-VEP' No 3588 catches the early-evening light as it enters **Rochester** on a slow Dover–Victoria service on 8 August 1998. *Roger Palmer*

Title page: On 22 May 2004 'Greyhound' '4-CIG' No 1312 pulls out of **St Denys** with the 09.47 from Southampton to Portsmouth Harbour. Before the summer was out Class 450 'Desiros' would take over this service, consigning these venerable units to history. *Roger Palmer*

First published 2006

ISBN (10) 0 7110 3108 8
ISBN (13) 978 0 7110 3108 1

Published by Ian Allan Publishing

an imprint of Ian Allan Publishing Ltd, Hersham, Surrey KT12 4RG
Printed in England by Ian Allan Printing Ltd, Hersham, Surrey KT12 4RG

Code: 0605/B1

Visit the Ian Allan Publishing website at www.ianallanpublishing.com

in service throughout the country concluded that the 'Greyhound' '4-CIGs' (numbered in the early 13xx series) operated out of Waterloo by South West Trains could accrue the highest mileage before going into works for repair. These were the very units condemned when new for looking a bit dated and latterly by the media for having doors that passengers had to open and close for themselves. It was probably significant that even in the spring of 2004, when Class 450 'Desiro' and Class 458 'Juniper' units were used regularly in service, these didn't seem to be trusted on anything beyond the Waterloo–Basingstoke or Waterloo–Alton services and, in the case of the 'Junipers', got no further than Reading. Meanwhile the reliable old '4-CEPs', '4-CIGs', and '4-VEPs' carried on regardless, and it was not uncommon, even as late as 2004, to see them charging along on fast trains to Southampton and on limited-stop services to Portsmouth Harbour.

South West Trains became the first train-operating company to eliminate slam-door stock from its services. Its last scheduled train ran on 26 May 2005, and a couple of specials ran on Saturdays 11 and 18 June, both named 'Seaside Slammers' and both running from Waterloo to Weymouth using celebrity 'VEP' No 3417 and one of the two newly-created '3-CIGs'. The other '3-CIG' worked on the Lymington branch, which, thanks to its 'heritage' status, has retained its slam-door stock. The newly styled Southern Railway ran its last scheduled slam-door train on a grey and dismal Friday 19 August 2005; this was the 17.17 service from Victoria to Eastbourne and Seaford, which, without any ado, became the very last slam-door train to serve Clapham Junction and East Croydon. Monday 5 September 2005 saw the last working of a scheduled slam door train on the South Eastern trains into Kent, after which a series of special trains were run as a farewell to these trusty old units.

This book is intended as a tribute to the three classes which served the old Southern Region of British Railways well for over 30 years. An attempt has been made to take a quantum leap backwards so that readers may make the connection between today's railway and that of the pre-Grouping era. Glamorous the 'CEPs', 'VEPs' and 'CIGs' were not; perhaps it was the fact that they replaced steam haulage on many routes that alienated many within the enthusiast fraternity. But they have become the very last link with the steam age, being the last survivors of what, during the 1950s and '60s became known as 'Eastleigh' stock, the origins of which went back to Oliver Bulleid's work on the original Southern Railway in the 1940s — or perhaps even before, some might argue! Contrasting with what has replaced them, they allowed travellers enough room to fidget, move their elbows without disrupting others and stretch their legs. There was also adequate space for luggage.

The book has been arranged in a broadly geographical sequence from east to west, Parkstone being the furthest point west I ever reached when photographing slam-door stock. Of the various books consulted, the appropriate volumes published by Middleton Press proved useful, while the following titles in particular helped fill some gaps in my somewhat scant knowledge:

The London, Brighton & South Coast Railway by C. Hamilton Ellis (Ian Allan, 1960)
The South Eastern & Chatham Railway by O. S. Nock (Ian Allan, 1961)
The London & South Western Railway by O. S. Nock (Ian Allan, 1965)
British Joint Lines by H. C. Casserley (Ian Allan, 1968)
A Regional History of the Railways of Great Britain, Volume 3: Greater London by H. P. White (David & Charles, 1971)
Southern Electric Album by Alan Williams (Ian Allan, 1977)
Southampton's Railways by Bert Moody (Waterfront Publications, 1992)
London, Brighton & South Coast Railway — Images of Railways by John Minnis (Tempus Publishing, 1999)

In conclusion I should like to thank all those who have helped me in creating this book, especially the late Brenda Masterman, for her encouragement on the editorial side, Paul Griffin, who advised me on some of the workings I had photographed, and to Peter Waller of Ian Allan Publishing, who made the whole book happen.

Roger Palmer
Chiswick
March 2006

When the Tonbridge–Hastings main line was electrified in 1985 British Railways marketed the new service as the 1066 route and painted the '4-CEP' units destined to work it in what became known as 'Jaffa Cake' livery. This colour scheme was subsequently extended to units working services throughout much of Kent and became popular with enthusiasts and the general public alike, but by the early 1990s sightings became rarer as more units started to appear in Network SouthEast colours. Here we see '4-CEP' No 1612 passing **Hither Green** on a Charing Cross–Dover service on 31 March 1990. *Catherine Masterman*

The old Southern Railway and its successor, British Railways Southern Region, would often use parts of earlier stock in the construction of more up-to-date vehicles. Old underframes dating back to the 1930s were used on stock built in the 1950s, old motors were used in sets built in the 1980s, and so on. One of the major criticisms of the '4-CEPs' and '4-CIGs' — and of the '4-REPs' and '4-TCs', which were direct contemporaries — was that old coaches built for locomotive haulage were inserted into these sets and passed off as new.

It may well be that re-forming of units has eliminated all but a handful of the oldest vehicles, but it was still possible in the early 1990s to take a ride on one of the suburban '4-EPB' units, based on an underframe which dated back to the 1940s; maybe No 5228 — seen in the later BR standard passenger colours of blue and grey at **Chislehurst** in March 1990 while on a Charing Cross–Orpington service — was one of them. *Catherine Masterman*

Immediately to the north of **Orpington** a maze of tracks carried stock from sidings — as well as fast expresses and stoppers — into the station area. Once past the station, trains from London very quickly found themselves on a double-track section only as they hurtled through leafy countryside on their way to Tonbridge and beyond. Here, in March 1990, '4-CEP' No 1618 stops to pick up passengers on its way from Charing Cross to Hastings. *Catherine Masterman*

The South Eastern Railway opened its line from Gravesend as far as **Strood** in February 1845 and extended it to Maidstone West in June 1856, thus allowing through running from Kent's county town to Charing Cross. By 1922 an erratic service of through trains was provided, but electrification of the line through Strood to Maidstone West and Gillingham in July 1939 enabled more trains to be run, at regular intervals. By 1947 a half-hourly service was provided south of Strood, alternate trains running to Charing Cross, but these had ceased by the 1970s, Maidstone East getting the through trains to Victoria and Strood's London service running instead to/from Gillingham. Here '4-CEP' No 1520 enters Strood with a train from Maidstone West on 9 September 1998. The bridge in the background carries the London, Chatham & Dover Railway's main line through Bromley South, and the connecting line between the erstwhile rivals goes off to the left of the picture. *Roger Palmer*

The station at **Cuxton** stands quietly on the banks of the Medway, the only sound being of water lapping gently against any boats moored there. The tranquility was disturbed only briefly four times an hour when trains passed through; here '4-CEP' No 1582 on a Maidstone West–Strood service draws to a halt on 29 August 1998. *Roger Palmer*

Time was when ageing steam engines were sent out to grass on some quiet branch line or byway before being retired, but times change. As often as not ageing electric stock carries on in much the same way as before whilst new trains are introduced on the quieter lines such as those from Sittingbourne to Sheerness, Strood to Paddock Wood or Guildford to Ascot. Even as late as April 2004 '4-CEPs', some nearly half a century old, could be seen on fast, limited-stop services from Waterloo to Portsmouth Harbour and on the occasional Victoria–Ramsgate working. By contrast the Sheerness and Maidstone West branches had by 1999 gained newer Class 508 stock from Merseyside. On 14 March 1998 '4-CEP' No 1551 enters **Maidstone West** with a Medway Valley train from Strood. *Catherine Masterman*

With the long-closed Battersea Power Station standing as a brooding silent witness to all around, a '4-CEP' passes **Wandsworth Road** with a train to Canterbury West from Victoria on 18 November 1995. To the left of the picture is the line which carries South London-line trains from London Bridge through Battersea Park and on to Victoria, while just beyond is the goods-only railway bringing freight to and from the West London line through the maze of junctions between here and Clapham Junction. *Catherine Masterman*

Herne Hill is where the London, Chatham & Dover Railway's line from Victoria was joined by that from the City of London via Ludgate Hill and Holborn Viaduct. Back in the mid-/late 19th century trains came in over this section from Hendon on the Midland Railway and from Hatfield on the Great Northern Railway, providing railway enthusiasts and observers with added interest as well as bringing a splash of colour to the scene.

By the 1990s their successors, in the form of Thameslink services, were coming in from Luton past the site of Ludgate Hill and through Blackfriars on their way to Sutton. Here, on 23 September 1995, a train from Victoria to Ramsgate passes over the junction, the line north towards Blackfriars being out of sight behind the train. *Roger Palmer*

Above: En route to its next stop at Bromley South, '4-CEP' No 1571 heads through **Kent House** with a Victoria–Maidstone East service on 6 November 1995. The plethora of bright-red lamp-posts indicates that this was the era of Network SouthEast, when such things spread across the system from March to Ramsgate and East Anglia to Oxford; since then colours, if not considerably faded, have been a little more sombre. *Roger Palmer*

Right: Eurostar excepted, all the trains at the turn of the 20th/21st centuries stop at **Bromley South**. On the golden autumn morning of 18 November 1995 '4-CEP' No 1507 prepares to call with a Victoria–Maidstone East service. *Roger Palmer*

Left: On 1 June 1874 the London, Chatham & Dover Railway opened a line from Otford Junction to Maidstone, an extension to Ashford opening on 1 July 1884. On the initial stretch of line is **Borough Green & Wrotham**, where on 3 September 2004, one of the last '4-CEPs' in service, No 1699, is seen paying a call with the 13.18 train from Victoria to Canterbury West. The unit's livery indicates earlier service with South West Trains.
Roger Palmer

Above: **Lenham** station is typical of those found on the section between Maidstone East and Ashford, but unlike those at Bearstead, Hollingbourne and Harrietsham it is built of red brick, similar to that used at Charing. In 2004 it was served by one stopping train an hour from Victoria but was also passed at speed by trains from Cannon Street to Ashford. Calling on 20 August 2004 is '4-VEP' No 3454, on a service for Canterbury West. *Roger Palmer*

Left: Ever since the station at Hothfield closed in November 1959 **Charing** has been the penultimate station on the London, Chatham & Dover Railway's extension from Maidstone East to Ashford, which opened in 1884. On 20 March 1995 '4-CEP' No 1597 draws to a halt with the 11.15 Victoria–Canterbury West service before proceeding towards the junction at Ashford and on to its destination. *Roger Palmer*

Above: Elevated signalboxes are something of a rarity in Southern England. Clapham Junction and Epsom each had one, but both disappeared during the 1990s. That at **Canterbury West** was still *in situ* on 4 October 1997, when '4-VEP' No 3574 was photographed entering the station with headcode appropriate to its next run to Victoria via Maidstone East; the unit had arrived a few minutes earlier on a down service before crossing over to the east of the station in readiness for its return journey. *Catherine Masterman*

17

Above: Despite boasting four platform faces, **Rochester** station had only two in regular use on Saturday 14 September 1996, when '4-VEP' No 3587 was photographed calling with a late-afternoon stopping service from Victoria to Dover Priory. *Catherine Masterman*

Right: The red lamp-posts were a principal feature of stations during the Network SouthEast era, between 1986 and railway privatisation in the mid-1990s. They were still in evidence at **Chatham** on 19 September 1998, when '4-CEP' No 1611 was photographed leaving on a Victoria–Dover Priory stopping service. *Catherine Masterman*

Above: Junction for lines from Victoria to Ramsgate and Dover, **Faversham** has been an important railway centre since the days of the London, Chatham & Dover Railway. An engine shed (in the 'V' of the junction of the two lines) remained open until electrification in 1959 and was still standing on 3 March 1995, when '4-CEP' No 1546 was photographed on a Victoria–Dover service. *Catherine Masterman*

Right: On the same day '4-CIG' No 1871 is seen entering **Faversham** on an afternoon fast service from Dover. Visible in the background is Faversham Junction, with the Ramsgate line veering off to the left and the main line to Dover to the right. *Catherine Masterman*

Above: Having started from Blackfriars instead of Victoria due to 'essential engineering work', '4-CEP' No 1580 calls at **Herne Bay** on a stopping service to Ramsgate on 2 April 1994. *Catherine Masterman*

Right: In the 19th century **Ramsgate** was served by two rival railways — the London, Chatham & Dover and the South Eastern. The former's station — Ramsgate Harbour — was served by trains from the junction at Faversham travelling by way of Herne Bay and Broadstairs, whereas the latter had a station known as Ramsgate Town, where trains from Minster terminated; there was also a branch from Ramsgate Town to Margate Sands, operated by the South Eastern Railway. The Southern Railway tidied things up by building a new stretch of line enabling passengers from the North Kent resorts of Herne Bay and Whitstable to travel via Margate, Broadstairs, Dumpton Park and Ramsgate to Minster, Deal or Dover. Stylish new stations were built at Ramsgate and Margate, the former being visible in the background of this March 1995 picture of '4-CEP' No 1553 heading towards Minster, Ashford and Maidstone East on its way to Victoria. *Catherine Masterman*

Above: According to a map produced by *The Railway Magazine* the line running southwards from Minster through **Sandwich** (opened in July 1847) terminated at Deal. It was not until 1881, after much wrangling between the South Eastern Railway and the London, Chatham & Dover Railway, that agreement was reached to run a joint line between Dover and Deal. Thus the Dover & Deal Joint Railway became the only line in Kent to be jointly owned by the two rivals. In rather more settled times, on 14 April 1995, '4-CEP' No 1507 arrives at Sandwich on a service from Margate to Charing Cross. *Catherine Masterman*

Left: On 13 September 1997 '4-CEP' No 1511 emerges from Priory Tunnel and draws into **Dover Priory** station on a fast service from London Victoria. Just beyond Charlton Tunnel (just visible in the distance) is Buckland Junction, where the ex-Dover & Deal Joint line joins the main line from Faversham and Canterbury East. *Catherine Masterman*

Right: In 1861, upon completion of its line from Faversham, the London, Chatham & Dover Railway gained the best route from London to Dover. The principal intermediate station was **Canterbury East**, which boasted an overall roof that in certain weather conditions made the place seem like a wind tunnel. In 1958 rather austere canopies were provided, which have latterly given way to the more decorative style seen on 29 September 1996 as '4-CEP' No 1590 calls on a stopping service from Victoria to Dover Priory. The bright-red lamp-posts were a common feature of Network SouthEast stations prior to the privatisation of Britain's railways in the mid-1990s. *Roger Palmer*

Right: A Dover–Charing Cross train led by '4-VEP' No 3805 negotiates the sharp curve at **Tonbridge** on 12 October 1997. It has just left what is believed to be the longest section of straight line in Britain — that between Leigh and Ashford, on the ex-South Eastern Railway line from Redhill. *Catherine Masterman*

Above: On what had once been the London & Croydon Railway, **Honor Oak Park** was opened in 1886, many years after the original concern had amalgamated with the London, Brighton & South Coast Railway. Over the years the station became a popular venue for photographers on the 'Brighton' and its successor, the Southern Railway. Here we see '4-CIG' No 1831 sprinting along the fast line towards London Bridge with the 10.02 from Horsham on 11 April 2005. *Roger Palmer*

Right: The London, Brighton & South Coast and the London, Chatham & Dover railways shared a station at **Victoria**. The latter's facilities were on the east side and are represented by today's Platforms 1-8, the tracks being visible on the extreme left of this picture, taken on 29 June 1996. Entering the station is a fast train from Brighton headed by '4-CIG' unit No 1906. *Catherine Masterman*

Left: Claiming to be Britain's busiest railway station, **Clapham Junction** sees hardly a minute go by during daylight hours without a train approaching or departing from one of its 16 operating platforms. In spite of its size and its multiplicity of tracks its basic function is quite simple: trains from Waterloo head towards the Thames riverside towns of Putney, Chiswick, Richmond, Staines and Windsor or take the more southerly route through Woking then on to Portsmouth, Salisbury or Southampton, whilst trains from Victoria simply glide through on their way to the Sussex coast. In addition the West London line creeps into the station using Platform 2 (out of sight to the left of this picture) and under the main lines to get into Platform 17, seen on the extreme right as '4-CIG' No 1833 heads an early-evening Victoria–Southampton train away from Platform 13 on 21 July 2003. *Roger Palmer*

Above: Once such a common sight on the London, Brighton & South Coast Railway, 'scalloped' station canopies are slowly but surely being replaced by a more plain and functional design. Probably the largest station to retain them is **Purley**, which plays host to stopping trains to Tattenham Corner, Caterham and Horsham. Longer-distance trains simply race through, as '4-CIG' No 1734, bound for Victoria on a service from Brighton via Redhill, demonstrates on 20 March 1999. *Roger Palmer*

There has been a station serving **Merstham** since December 1841. Moved about a mile to the north (to its present site) in October 1843, it was rebuilt in 1905. A century later, on 22 April 2005, '4-VEP' No 3482 enters the station on the 10.02 Horsham–London Bridge service. *Roger Palmer*

Originally part of the London & Brighton Railway's main line, opened in July 1841, the section between Redhill and Stoats Nest, Coulsdon, was sold to the South Eastern Railway before completion. Thereafter until 1900 the LBSC and the SER were obliged to share the tracks all the way from here to London Bridge, and each company was dependent on the goodwill of the other to ensure that its passengers were treated to a decent service. In April 1900 the LBSCR opened its 'Quarry' line bypassing Redhill, giving it an independent, fast route from Stoats Nest Junction to Sussex and the South Coast; by this time the SER had opened its own route through Orpington and Sevenoaks to Tonbridge. Here '4-CIG' No 1733 leaves **Redhill** bound for Victoria on a service from Bognor Regis on 17 April 1999. *Roger Palmer*

Left: **Earlswood**, on the slow lines between Redhill and Horley, is another station to retain the 'scalloped' canopies favoured by the London, Brighton & South Coast Railway. On 17 April 1999 '4-VEP' No 3436 calls with a Horsham–London Bridge service. Sadly for those with an eye for history and their heritage, these old canopies were replaced about a year later, as part of station 'improvements'. At least the roof no longer leaked! *Roger Palmer*

Below left: One of the more important stations between Redhill and Gatwick Airport is **Horley**, where there is quite a sizable settlement. At the time of writing (2006) it retains four platforms, although only two are in regular use. It plays host to Victoria/London Bridge and Tunbridge Wells–Horsham services as well as a few trains to/from Littlehampton via the Arun Valley line. Here '4-VEP' No 3517 departs with a Victoria–Horsham service on Saturday 20 February 1999. *Roger Palmer*

Right: By 2005 **Horsham** had become one of the last stations to see slam-door stock, two such trains per hour ending their journeys there. One of these was from London Bridge, traveling by way of Merstham, Redhill and Horley; the other, from Tunbridge Wells, went via Tonbridge, Edenbridge and Redhill. On 6 May 2005 '4-CIG' No 1862 arrives on the 15.33 service from London Bridge. In the background can be seen the junction of the Dorking and Three Bridges lines, as well as Horsham's splendid art-deco signalbox. *Roger Palmer*

Left: In common with many other wayside stations on Britain's main-line railways, **Wivelsfield** boasts no station buildings of any architectural merit. By 2006 the only original waiting shelter to survive was that on the down side. That on the up side, swept away by 2000, is seen here on 20 March 1999 hiding behind '4-CIG' No 1738 on an Eastbourne–Victoria service. The train's next stop will be Haywards Heath. *Roger Palmer*

Above: Still in Network SouthEast colours on 20 March 1999, '4-CIG' No 1805 gallops up the Brighton main line towards **Keymer Junction** with a Littlehampton–Victoria train. The tracks in the foreground lead to Lewes, Eastbourne and Hastings. *Roger Palmer*

Above: Serving a northern suburb of Eastbourne, **Hampden Park** has the novel distinction of seeing the same train pass its platforms twice. This is because trains from Victoria or Brighton to Hastings have to travel via Eastbourne and reverse, the direct line between Polegate and Pevensey having closed in 1969. Paying a call on 12 August 1989 is '4-CIG' No 1255 on a service from Hastings to Brighton. *Catherine Masterman*

Right: In common with all South Coast termini except Seaford, **Eastbourne** boasts extensive sidings for the overnight berthing of units. In the steam era it had an engine shed, where in early British Railways days one could see ancient ex-Brighton engines, many last survivors of types which had disappeared from the general scene. During the last 10-15 years of slam-door operation '4-CIGs' dominated, with the occasional '4-VEP' paying a call. On 4 May 1998 '4-CIG' No 1856 was recorded departing on a Hastings–Victoria service. *Catherine Masterman*

Above: Prior to 1969 it was possible for trains from either Brighton or Victoria to bypass Eastbourne on their way to or from Hastings; until then a triangle of lines linking Polegate, Willingdon Junction (just north of Hampden Park) and Stone Cross Junction (where the line forming the third side of the triangle joined from Polegate) permitted far greater flexibility of operation and the potential for a faster service west of Hastings, but this was not to last. On 12 May 2001 '4-CIG' No 1734 enters **Pevensey & Westham** station on a Brighton–Hastings service which would have reversed at Eastbourne. *Catherine Masterman*

Right: The coast line between Brighton and Portsmouth was opened in stages from May 1840, when the LBSCR reached Shoreham. No 1408, one of the 11 '3-COP' units used exclusively on what were known latterly as Coastway services, is seen leaving **Hove** on 21 November 1998 on a Littlehampton–Brighton working. *Roger Palmer*

Left: Built as a single-storey building in 1846 and rebuilt in the 1860s, **Angmering** underwent several extensions to its platforms over the years to accommodate ever-increasing lengths of train. Here, on 14 August 2004, '4-CIG' No 1741 calls with the 13.12 Bognor Regis–Victoria service. *Roger Palmer*

Above: **Littlehampton** was the terminus of a branch from Ford Junction which opened in August 1863. A spur from the coast line, opened in 1887, allowed direct services to be run to/from Brighton and, via the Cliftonville spur, the main Brighton–Victoria line. The station was completely rebuilt in the early 1990s but retained its semaphore signalling controlled by an LBSC signalbox (just beyond the platform ends), seen as the 14.00 service from Brighton, worked by '4-CIG' No 1708, arrives on 14 August 2004. *Roger Palmer*

After a convoluted pre-history, which included plans to bring the railway from Midhurst via a point to the east of the present station at Chichester, **Bognor Regis** finally got its railway in 1864, from a junction with the LBSCR's coast line at Barnham. This arrangement enabled Bognor trains to run direct to Victoria or Brighton. The early history of the station was fraught with drama, as the first building was blown down during a ferocious gale in 1897, and the second burned down only a few years later. The present station was built in 1902 and first saw electric trains in 1937. On 17 August 2004 a lunchtime train for Littlehampton, with headcode 67 already in place, awaits departure time. *Roger Palmer*

The inspiration for taking a photograph at **Billingshurst** came from an illustration by well-known LBSCR chronicler H. M. Madgewick, published in R. C. Riley's splendid 1967 volume *Brighton Line Album*, featuring one of William Stroudley's 'D1' 0-4-2 tanks. Times move on, and by 1993

Billingshurst was served by '4-CIGs' on an hourly headway from Chichester. Seen calling on 27 March is '4-CIG' No 1707, on the 11.06 Chichester–Victoria service. *Catherine Masterman*

Time was when extensive sidings existed just to the west of **Chichester** station, on a site known as Westgate Fields. Many of these disappeared during the years following World War 2, those on the down side of the main running line being eliminated completely. The sidings on the up side remained *in situ*, rusting away until 2004, when a new freight terminal opened. On 13 August 2004 '4-VEP' No 3485 approaches from the west on the 12.18 Southampton–Littlehampton service. *Roger Palmer*

With jolly faces hanging out of the windows in traditional railtour style, blue celebrity 'VEP' No 3417 passes **Vauxhall** on 18 June 2005 on the very last passenger-carrying slam-door working from Waterloo. The train was the 'Seaside Slammer' special to Weymouth, and as if to mark this historic occasion its occupants enjoyed unbroken sunshine throughout the day. *Roger Palmer*

Above: Opened in November 1877 and for a short time used as a stopping-place for a London & North Western Railway service from Willesden Junction, the station known originally as Queen's Road, Battersea, had its name changed on 12 May 1980 to **Queenstown Road**. During the hot and sunny evening rush-hour of 4 August 1998 '4-CEP' No 1517 whisks past on the 17.20 Portsmouth & Southsea–Waterloo service, due to reach its destination at 18.48. *Roger Palmer*

Above right: Opened along with the rest of the line from Nine Elms to Woking in May 1838, **Wimbledon** was completely rebuilt in 1929, making it easier for passengers to make the connection with the District Railway's trains to Earl's Court and the Underground system. Early one morning in June 1988 '4-BIG' No 2001 is seen heading an up Bournemouth-line train through Platform 6 on its way to Waterloo. The second vehicle in the train is the buffet car. *Roger Palmer*

Right: Having the distinction at the time of writing (March 2006) of being the latest railway built in London's southern suburbs, the section of line from Motspur Park opened as far as **Tolworth** on 29 May 1938 and about a year later was extended to Chessington South. This opened on 28 May 1939; World War 2 prevented the Southern Railway from carrying it further to Leatherhead, as originally planned. By the mid-1980s sliding-door stock was the norm, but for a short period in the early months of 2004 the 18.22 from Waterloo was worked by slam-door units such as '4-VEP' No 3404, seen at Tolworth on 18 May; timetable changes later that month would put a stop to such workings. Note the ultra-modern-looking station canopies — a feature on this line. *Roger Palmer*

Opened at the same time as Wimbledon, **Surbiton** was originally the station for the ancient town of Kingston-upon-Thames. The elders of Kingston rejected the idea of a main line passing through, forcing the London & Southampton Railway (precursor of the London & South Western Railway) to go through Surbiton, which prospered as a consequence — much to the chagrin of Kingston! On a June evening in 1988 '4-VEP' No 3072 is seen hammering along on a fast Waterloo–Portsmouth Harbour service, overtaking one of the then new Class 455 units on a down stopper, to Guildford via Cobham. *Roger Palmer*

Weybridge was one of the original stations of the London & Southampton Railway, opened in May 1838 between Nine Elms and Woking and subsequently extended westwards through Basingstoke, Winchester and on to Southampton. Quadrupling of the tracks was a piecemeal affair carried out during the latter part of the 19th century and by 1904 had reached Worting Junction (to the west of Basingstoke). This enabled fast running of expresses such as this Waterloo–Portsmouth Harbour service, led by '4-CIG' No 1398 and destined to take the 'old' route by way of Winchester and Fareham, on 13 July 2004. *Roger Palmer*

Above: Seen at **Woking**, where the Portsmouth Direct line parts company with the South Western main line, on 30 March 2004 is '4-CEP' No 2311. The train had started its journey at Poole, stopping at all stations to Southampton, where it would have waited for no less than 23 minutes to recuperate before heading off again, this time with a few stops to Basingstoke; from there it would have taken the fast tracks to gallop up to Woking, from where it would enjoy another fast run to Clapham Junction and Waterloo. *Roger Palmer*

Right: Until the renaming of West Weybridge as Byfleet & New Haw, **Worplesdon** station was the last in an alliterative sequence of six 'Ws' starting with Walton-on-Thames. The building style is similar to that employed at New Milton and Hinton Admiral. Captured passing at speed on Saturday 31 May 2003 was the 07.55 Portsmouth & Southsea–Waterloo service, led by 40-year-old '4-CEP' unit No 1612. *Roger Palmer*

Opened in 1845 as a branch from Woking, **Guildford** became a through station in 1849, when an extension to Godalming was opened by the LSWR and a through line from Redhill to Reading started business by what became the South Eastern & Chatham Railway. The Godalming line was further extended southwards by way of Haslemere and Petersfield to a junction with the London, Brighton & South Coast Railway's line to Portsmouth at Havant; this was opened in 1859 amidst violent controversy and provided the competing London & South Western Railway with the fastest route to Portsmouth from

London. In 1865 the LBSCR opened a line from Horsham, joining the LSWR's Portsmouth line at Peasmarsh Junction, while a further railway, entering Guildford from the north — from Surbiton by way of Cobham — opened in 1885. Here, looking northwards on 31 May 2003, we see '4-CEP' No 1550 approaching the station on the original line from Woking with a Waterloo–Portsmouth Harbour service. On the left can be seen the line to Aldershot and Reading, whilst coming into the picture from the right is the line from Cobham. *Roger Palmer*

Anyone wishing to visit Normandy without taking a passport is advised to travel by train to the nearby village of **Wanborough**, between Guildford and Aldershot. In the early 2000s this station saw two stopping trains an hour, as well as trains between Reading and Gatwick racing through non-stop.

It was to lose its slam-door stock early in 2004, but when photographed on 31 May 2003 it was host to '4-CEP' No 2317 on a mid-day Ascot–Guildford service. *Roger Palmer*

Left: **Godalming** was reached by a branch from Woking in 1849, and 10 years later, in a speculative venture by contractors, was incorporated into the Portsmouth Direct line through Haslemere and Petersfield to Havant, where a junction was made with the existing LBSCR coast line from Chichester. The old terminus station at Godalming remained in use for goods traffic until January 1969. Here '4-VEP' No 3559 calls at the 1859 station with a Waterloo–Portsmouth Harbour working on Saturday 15 May 2004. *Roger Palmer*

Above: Early in the 21st century **Haslemere** was served by four trains an hour from Waterloo during the middle part of the day, of which one terminated, two carried on to Portsmouth Harbour, stopping only at Petersfield, Havant and the three stations within the boundaries of Portsmouth, and the fourth worked all stations to Portsmouth & Southsea. Just after mid-day on 23 April 2004 '4-CEP' No 2317 draws into Platform 2, its '73' headcode indicating that this is as far as it will go. *Roger Palmer*

Left: The stations at Whitley, Liphook and Rowlands Castle all had similar buildings and waiting-shelters, and all three were served by an hourly service from Waterloo. On Saturday 15 May 2004 'Greyhound' '4-CIG' No 1309 calls at **Liphook** with a service from Portsmouth Harbour. *Roger Palmer*

Above: On 4 September 2004 the only slam-door trains running on the Portsmouth Direct line south of Haslemere were the hourly stoppers to/from Portsmouth & Southsea. Here an eight-car train led by 'Greyhound' '4-CIG' No 1319 calls at **Rowlands Castle**. *Roger Palmer*

'Greyhound' '4-CIG' No 1311 approaches the junction with the line from Chichester and Brighton at **Havant** on a service from Waterloo to Portsmouth Harbour on 5 May 2003. This was the site of the infamous punch-up between navvies employed by the LSWR and the LBSCR, which attempted to prevent the former company from using its direct route via Guildford to Portsmouth.

After a running battle which saw sections of track removed and (presumably) many bloody noses and black eyes, the LSWR men were forced to retreat. However, within a month the matter was settled in the courts, allowing the LSWR to run its trains over the 'direct' line from Guildford and Godalming — much to the dismay of the LBSCR's officials. *Roger Palmer*

'4-CEP' No 1553, with three of its four carriages built in 1959 and one built in 1962, leads the 12.47 Portsmouth Harbour–Waterloo service into **Fratton** on 25 October 2003; it hardly looks to be within five months of being towed away for scrap, does it? Nevertheless, old age would finally catch up with it, and we next see it at Woking in March 2004 — see page 79.
Roger Palmer

In the early/mid-19th century Portsmouth could be reached by rather roundabout routes from London. The London & South Western Railway's route was effectively a branch off the London–Southampton line at Eastleigh, whilst the competing London, Brighton & South Coast Railway's service had to reverse at Brighton and trundle along the Sussex coast. The Brighton company met the LSWR by an end-on junction at **Cosham**, and the two companies operated jointly into Fratton and, eventually, Portsmouth Harbour.

By the early 2000s Cosham was served by trains originating from Cardiff, Southampton, Victoria and Waterloo. On 11 October 2003 '4-VEP' No 3576 calls with the 11.47 Southampton–Portsmouth Harbour service. *Roger Palmer*

At the turn of the 20th/21st centuries **Swanwick**, immediately to the west of Fareham, was graced with two stopping trains per hour during the day. One was the all-stations Portsmouth–Southampton, the other a service which during the 1990s carried the headcode 46 and ran from Victoria to Bournemouth, this being the furthest point west reached by the late and unlamented Connex South Central trains; this was cut back to Southampton in May 2001 and following the May 2004 timetable changes ran as a Littlehampton–Southampton train, its headcode changing from 46 to 36. (Bognor Regis gained a service with the headcode 46 at around the same time.) On the afternoon of Thursday 2 September 2004 the 14.18 Southampton–Littlehampton stops to do what little business was on offer. *Roger Palmer*

Above: **St Denys** is where the Portsmouth–Southampton line through Fareham joins the main line to Southampton from Waterloo. It was opened on its present site in March 1866, when the first part of the line to Portsmouth was opened, as far as Netley, replacing a small two-platform affair a short distance to the north. Originally known as Portswood, it was renamed in March 1876. Electric trains started running on the Southampton–Waterloo line in July 1967 in connection with the Bournemouth electrification project, but the line from Portsmouth was not electrified until 1990. Leaving the Portsmouth line on 2 September 2004 is '4-CIG' No 1874 on the 16.09 Littlehampton–Southampton service;

leading straight ahead towards the left of the picture is the main line to Waterloo. *Roger Palmer*

Right: During the late afternoon and early evening a service was run, invariably using slam-door trains, from Southampton to Winchester and back. With the estuary of the River Itchen as a background and headcode 94 in place 'Greyhound' '4-CIG' No 1309 passes the long-closed Bevois Park sidings as it approaches **St Denys** with the 16.19 Southampton–Winchester on 2 September 2004. *Roger Palmer*

Above: Some wag once referred to **Brookwood** as being the dead centre of Surrey, on account of the nearby cemetery. On 31 March 2003 '4-BEP' No 2325 calls with the 14.10 Waterloo–Basingstoke stopper — a service that would be converted to Class 450 'Desiro' operation before the year was out. Note the distinctive cupola on the down platform. *Roger Palmer*

Right: The opening of the line through **Aldershot** on 2 May 1870 enabled through-running of trains from Alton to Woking and Waterloo; previously trains from Alton ended up at Guildford, having travelled by way of Tongham. A spur linking the Waterloo line with the Guildford–Reading line was opened in 1879, and it is over this section that '4-CEP' No 1571 has worked during the early mid-summer evening of 21 June 2003 on its way from Guildford to Ascot. Following reversal here at Aldershot it will head northwards towards Ash Vale, where it will branch off the line to Woking and make its way through Frimley and on to Ascot. *Catherine Masterman*

There is very much an 'end of the line' feel about **Alton**, but for a time from 1903 passengers from Waterloo could continue their journey via the Meon Valley line to Fareham, the Mid-Hants line to Winchester or the light railway to Basingstoke. However, Basingstoke lost its service in 1932, while the Meon Valley line closed to passengers in 1955. Electric trains started running as far as Alton in July 1937, and at the turn of the 20th/21st centuries two trains per hour were provided, to/from Waterloo only, and an hourly service on Sundays.

Since the beginning of 2004 'Desiro' units had taken over from the trusty old slam-door trains on most services, but seen drawing to a halt at Platform 2 on Sunday 16 November 2003 is '4-BEP' No 2322, on a service which, due to engineering works on the main line west of Woking, had started from Guildford. Meanwhile the Mid-Hants line, closed in 1973, has been reopened as far as Alresford by preservationists and operates during the summer and on certain weekends during the winter months. *Roger Palmer*

Breaking the all-pervading quietude at **Winchfield** on 27 March 2002 is '4-CIG' No 1399 on an up Southampton-line fast train running where the stoppers usually go. This particular 'CIG' was one of the eight 'Greyhound' units which received carriages from redundant or withdrawn '4-CEP' units — in this case the second carriage from the front (from unit No 1595), which can easily be recognised by the aluminium frames to the windows. A complete '4-CEP' unit brings up the rear of the train. *Roger Palmer*

In common with New Malden, Esher, Walton-on-Thames, Farnborough and Winchfield, **Hook** boasted an island platform between the fast up and down running-lines. These were gradually taken out of use and in the case of Farnborough, Winchfield and Hook were completely erased from the scene; just look at the yawning gap between the platforms as a '4-BEP' calls with the 12.47 Basingstoke–Waterloo service on 24 March 2003. Note also the disused buffet car in the train's formation. *Roger Palmer*

Opened in 1839, **Basingstoke** grew in importance when the Great Western Railway opened its line from Reading in 1848, since when there has always been much traffic between the (G)WR and SR. At the beginning of the 21st century Virgin CrossCountry trains from Scotland and the North of England used this line to reach Southampton, Bournemouth or Poole, whilst Freightliner trains from Southampton also use the connection. On a stiflingly hot 3 August 2003 '4-CIG' No 1399 leaves with the Sunday 11.50 Waterloo–Bournemouth train. *Roger Palmer*

Above: **Winchester**, the ancient capital of Wessex, once boasted two stations, one on a line from Didcot over the Berkshire and Hampshire downs through Newbury and Whitchurch and joining the LSWR line at Shawford Junction *en route* to Southampton, the other on the original London & Southampton Railway, shown here on 6 May 2002 as 'Greyhound' '4-CIG' No 1306 calls with a late-afternoon Waterloo–Portsmouth service. It was pressure from the burghers of Portsmouth, who didn't want an association with Southampton, that persuaded the existing railway to change its name to the London & South Western Railway. *Catherine Masterman*

Right: The importance of **Brockenhurst** as a railway centre grew from 1858, when it became the junction station for the Lymington branch, and increased when it became the starting-point for trains to Poole going by way of Ringwood, Wimborne and Broadstone on the 'old' main line following the opening of the direct line to Christchurch in 1888, giving the ever-growing town of Bournemouth a better, faster service to/from the east. On the late afternoon of 28 February 1995 a train from Waterloo heads into the setting sun as it makes its way to Bournemouth. *Catherine Masterman*

Above: Opened by an independent company in May 1858 and vested in the London & South Western Railway in March 1879, the Lymington branch had become the very last country branch line in Britain to be worked by steam traction by the time it was electrified as part of the Bournemouth-line electrification project in 1967. Goods facilities had long since disappeared by 12 September 2003, when '4-BEP' No 2325, which spent the day running up and down the line to and from the junction at Brockenhurst,

was photographed on an early-afternoon working drawing to a halt at **Lymington Pier** station. *Catherine Masterman*

Right: Almost two years later, on 9 July 2005, after the Lymington branch had gained 'Heritage' status, one of the newly formed '3-CIG' units, No 1498, is seen at **Lymington Junction** on its approach to Brockenhurst. *Catherine Masterman*

As was traditional with Southern electric units, a certain amount of renumbering took place due to reformations. Seen at **New Milton** on the 10.06 Poole–Waterloo service on the glorious morning of 12 September 2003, '4-CEP' No 2317 had been '4-BEP' No 2307 prior to losing its buffet car and gaining a carriage from withdrawn No 1538. *Catherine Masterman*

Until 1931 **Christchurch** was the junction for a railway that headed north through Hurn and ended up at Ringwood, on the 'old' main line linking Brockenhurst with Bournemouth and Poole. In the early 21st century the station saw two trains per hour in each direction, one of which was an all-stations to Southampton, running thence as a semi-fast to Waterloo. The train is seen leaving Christchurch in the early stages of its journey from Bournemouth on 14 September 2003, with '4-CEP' No 1550 doing the honours.
Catherine Masterman

Left: Time was when one could see trains from places as far apart as Sheffield, Bristol, Nottingham, Manchester, Bradford, Cleethorpes, Liverpool, Birmingham and Derby going through **Parkstone**. But time was when trains could travel from these places over the Somerset & Dorset line, until its closure in 1966. It joined the existing line from Bournemouth to Weymouth at Holes Bay Junction, to the west of Poole. Since the mass closures and cutbacks of the late 20th century the station sees only stopping trains such as the 12.06 Poole–Waterloo, worked on Monday 15 September 2003 by 'Greyhound' '4-CIG' No 1311. *Roger Palmer*

Above: One of the more melancholy sights of 2004/5 was the spectacle of the many scrap trains which hauled redundant units to various sites throughout the country. On 31 March 2004 '4-CEP' units Nos 1553 and 1563 are seen approaching **Woking** behind Class 67 No 67019, which was taking them on their last journey from Fratton to Immingham, where they would be cut up. *Roger Palmer*

Index of Locations

Although some were allocated to the Central section soon after they were built, the 4-CEPs had by 1989 been confined to the lines serving Kent and had become quite rare on the Central section. It therefore came as a surprise on 12 August to see a rather tatty-looking No 1542, still in 'Jaffa Cake' livery, passing through **Falmer** on a Hastings to Brighton service.
Catherine Masterman